AIR-CRAZY

Fascinating stories of Canadian women in the air

Photo: City of Vancouver Archives.

by

Elizabeth Gillan Muir

Another Chapter Publishing

Kanata, Ontario

Printed in Canada. Second printing 2016.

visit us at: www.anotherchapterpublishing.com

visit Elizabeth Muir at: www.lizmuir.ca

Cover photograph: City of Vancouver Archives
Cover and text background photograph: Roxanne McLaren

Library and Archives Canada Cataloguing in Publication

Cataloguing data available from Library and Archives Canada

INTRODUCTION

Did you know that many Canadian pilots are women?

Canadian women are even astronauts.

About 100 years ago, when airplanes were first invented, many people believed that women shouldn't fly in planes, not even as passengers. Flying was supposed to be only for men.

But many women in Canada desperately wanted to fly. They thought about it so much that they were called "air-crazy." Some women begged to go up in the air just for the ride. Other women worked hard to pay for flying lessons and find someone to teach them how to fly.

Eventually, women became pilots, stewardesses, flying instructors, and astronauts.

These are the stories of some of those courageous and determined women who contributed so much to the history of aviation in Canada.

OLIVE STARK

One of the first female airplane passengers in Canada

Olive Stark was born around 1877, before planes were even invented. When she grew up, Olive wanted to fly in an airplane, so on April 24, 1912, her husband, Billy, gave her a ride over Vancouver in his Curtiss Flyer plane. Olive was one of the very first women in Canada to fly in an airplane.

Billy bought his plane in California for $5,500, which would be about the same as spending $140,000 today. There was only one seat on Billy's airplane, so Olive sat on a board that Billy tied to one wing. She hung onto wires, and her legs dangled in the air.

Olive wore a pair of men's pants, called breeches, to keep her warm, which was considered as scandalous as flying. At that time people thought women should wear only dresses. It was very cold up in the air, even for the pilot, although the plane flew at only 40 miles per hour. Early planes had no covered cockpits and were wide open.

Olive flew with Billy many times, sometimes wearing a dress.

DID YOU KNOW?

When airplanes were first invented, the pilot lay flat on the plane. At that time, planes were like gliders. Very soon, planes had one or two seats. Early planes were made of wire, wood, and cloth. Today, planes are made of very strong metals.

1900 1910 1920 1930 1940

Olive and Billy in an early plane with two steering wheels. Olive was a passenger, not a second pilot. She never did learn how to fly an airplane.
Photo: City of Vancouver Archives.

1950 1960 1970 1980 1990 2000

ALYS MCKEY BRYANT

The first female pilot to fly a plane in Canada

Born in 1880, Alys McKey was so short she was nicknamed “Tiny.” She was also known as “The White Flyer” because she wore large white bloomers (pants) when she rode a bicycle.

Alys was an American school teacher, and taught home economics before she learned how to fly. She built and flew her own plane, even before she took flying lessons.

Alys and her husband, Johnny, flew over Victoria, British Columbia, on July 31 and August 1, 1913, to entertain the Prince of Wales and the Duke of York, King George V’s sons, who were visiting Canada that year. On July 31, Alys flew for sixteen minutes, 2,100 feet in the air, while Johnny flew 5,100 feet in the air.

Alys was the first female pilot to fly a plane in Canada.

DID YOU KNOW?

Commercial airplanes have flown as high as 60,000 feet, but generally large planes fly between 25,000 and 45,000 feet above the ground.

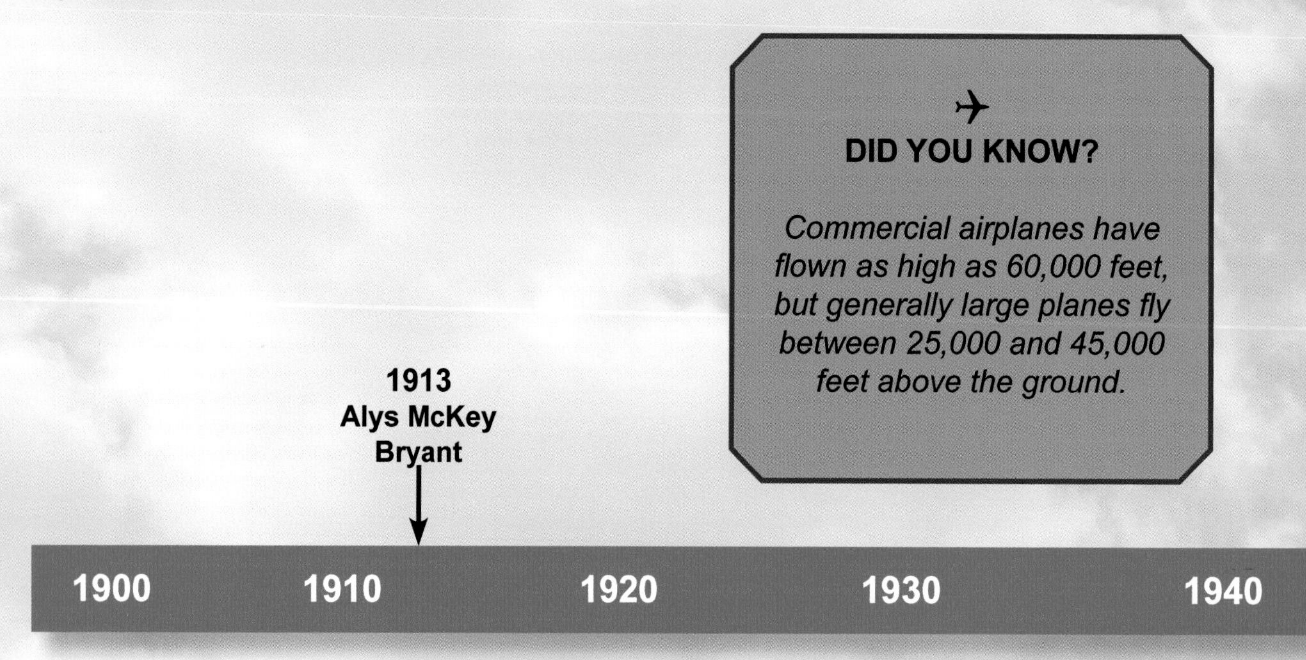

Alys in her plane, in the United States in 1913.
Photo: City of Vancouver Archives.

KATHERINE STINSON

The first pilot to fly airmail in Western Canada

Katherine Stinson, born in 1891, always looked younger than she was. She dressed in young girls' clothes and was called "The Flying Schoolgirl," even as an adult. Katherine originally wanted to be a musician, but found she could earn more money by flying airplanes at fairs, so she decided to become a pilot instead.

Katherine flew in a yellow biplane that was constructed from pieces of other planes that could no longer fly. People called it a "junk-shop hybrid." An American, Katherine flew across the United States, in China and Japan, and in Canada in Ontario and Alberta. She flew a bag of mail from Calgary to Edmonton in 1918, becoming the first airmail pilot in the Canadian west. During World War II, she flew to raise money for the Red Cross, and also drove an ambulance in France.

Katherine liked speed, whether in the air or on the ground. In 1918, she set a world record for driving a Fiat car in Edmonton at 45 miles an hour.

There is a full-sized model of Katherine's plane in the Alberta Aviation Museum in Edmonton, Alberta. It was built by fifteen volunteers, and took four years to build.

✈

DID YOU KNOW?

A biplane is an airplane which has two long wings, one placed above the other. "Bi", at the beginning of a word, means "two".

1900 1910 1920 1930 1940

Katherine Stinson (right) and her sister Marjorie in Katherine's plane. Marjorie was also a pilot. Their family owned a flying school in Texas. Photo: Smithsonian National Air and Space Museum.

MADGE GRAHAM

The first female airplane navigator in Canada

Born in 1882, Madge Graham flew on five-day trips with her husband, Stuart, over Quebec and Nova Scotia during 1919 and 1920. Stuart Graham was likely the first bush pilot in Canada.

Their airplane was named “La Vigilance” which means “watchfulness.” It was later used to watch for forest fires. Their plane was called a “flying boat”, because it took off and landed on water.

As the navigator, Madge sat at the very front of the plane in an open cockpit so she could watch where they were going. She got very wet when the plane took off and landed on the water. The plane was so noisy that Madge and Stuart couldn’t hear each other speak, so Madge rigged up a clothesline on the plane. They communicated by pinning messages on the line and sending them back and forth to each other.

Wherever they landed, people came to see Madge. Some women thought Madge was great. Other people thought Madge should be at home doing housework.

We can see their airplane in the Canada Aviation and Space Museum in Ottawa, Ontario.

✈

DID YOU KNOW?

Bush pilots fly over forests to look for forest fires. They fly people and materials to places where there are no roads, especially in the north.

1919
Madge Graham

1900 **1910** **1920** **1930** **1940**

Madge Graham sitting in the front of "La Vigilance." The plane is being launched (pushed) into the water.
Photo: Canada Aviation and Space Museum.

1950 1960 1970 1980 1990 2000

EILEEN VOLLICK

The first Canadian female pilot

Born in Wiarton, Ontario in 1908, Eileen Vollick was a beauty queen before she learned how to fly. When she was 18, she parachuted from the wing of an airplane into Burlington Bay at Hamilton, Ontario, but she really wanted to be a pilot.

On March 13, 1928, when she was 19, Eileen got her pilot's licence from the Jack Elliot Flying School. It was winter, and the cockpit was open, so Eileen wore a fur-lined flying suit. She sat on cushions to see out of the window because she was so short.

She was the first woman in Canada to get her licence. At that time, boys could get a licence at the age of 17, but girls had to wait until they were older.

Eileen said that people who didn't fly couldn't know how beautiful it was in the air. She liked to do spins, loops, and other stunts in her airplane, just like an aerobatic pilot.

The Wiarton/Keppel Airport named their terminal, the "Eileen Vollick Terminal", after her. It was the first Canadian airport to be named after a woman.

Eileen Vollick Hopkin, the first Canadian woman to earn a pilot's licence. Photo: Canada Aviation and Space Museum.

✈

DID YOU KNOW?

On August 2, 2008, a postage stamp showing Eileen in a Curtiss Jenny airplane was issued on the 100th anniversary of her birth.

1950 1960 1970 1980 1990 2000

LOUISE JENKINS

The first woman in Canada to own a plane

Louise Jenkins, born in 1890, took flying lessons in Quebec and Florida, and was the first female pilot in Prince Edward Island.

Louise was also the first Canadian woman to own her own plane. She bought a red and silver "Puss Moth" in 1932. That year, she set a record when she flew from Montreal to Charlottetown in less than five hours.

Louise flew sick people to hospital, and took part in flying demonstrations. She loved flying so much that she flew clean laundry to her son, Jackie, at his boarding school, and clean clothes to her daughter, Joan, when she was at summer camp.

Louise was called the "Daring Lady Flyer", but some people in Prince Edward Island thought she should be staying at home instead of flying.

Louise and her husband, Dr. Jack Jenkins, built the first airport in Prince Edward Island on their own land at Upton Farm.

✈

DID YOU KNOW?

There are a number of postage stamps of Canadian female pilots in this book. How many can you find?

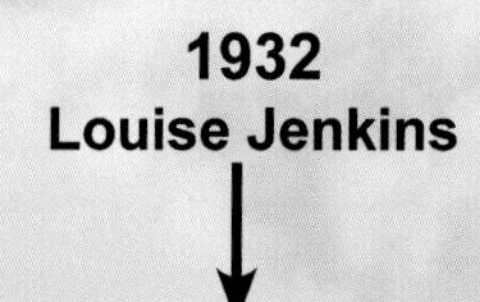

1900 1910 1920 1930 1940

Louise Jenkins with her airplane.
Photo: Royal Aviation Museum of Western Canada.

LUCILE GRANT and PAT ECCLESTON

The first stewardesses to fly with a Canadian airline

When we fly in an airplane, male and female flight attendants look after us. They serve us food, and make sure we are comfortable and safe.

Trans-Canada Airlines (TCA) started in 1937. At that time, passenger flying could be a terrifying experience. The planes were small, often having only ten seats. Aisle ceilings were low, and passengers couldn't stand up if they were tall. Often passengers had to put on oxygen masks. The planes couldn't fly in bad weather.

Trans-Canada Airlines (now known as Air Canada) thought that if women weren't afraid to fly, business men would fly, too. So, in 1938, TCA hired their first flight attendants, then called stewardesses.

Lucile Grant, born in 1910, and Pat Eccelston, born in 1916, were the first two stewardesses on Trans-Canada Airlines. At that time, stewardesses had to follow very strict requirements. They had to be unmarried, less than 30 years of age, and between 5'2" and 5'6" in height. They couldn't weigh more than 125 pounds. They couldn't wear glasses, and had to have short hair.

DID YOU KNOW?

The first stewardesses had to be registered nurses, because sometimes passengers got airsick.

Although the requirements were strict, women thought it was an exciting job. By 1940, there were more than 28 stewardesses working with Trans-Canada Airlines.

Today, both men and women are flight attendants.

1938
Lucile Grant
Pat Eccleston

1900 1910 1920 1930 1940

Lucile Grant and Pat Eccleston, the first two stewardesses on Trans-Canada Airlines, later called Air Canada. Photo: Canada Aviation and Space Museum.

1950 1960 1970 1980 1990 2000

ELSIE MACGILL

The first woman in the world to design an airplane that flew

Born in 1905, Elsie MacGill was from Vancouver, British Columbia. She was the first woman to become an aeronautical engineer, and designed the Maple Leaf Trainer II airplane in 1938. Unfortunately, Elsie could never be a pilot herself, because she had polio and used two canes to walk.

Elsie MacGill, the world's first female airplane designer.
Photo: Canada Aviation and Space Museum.

In 1939, Elsie became the chief engineer at Canada Car & Foundry (Can Car) in Montreal, Quebec. She was put in charge of building 1,450 Hawker Hurricane airplanes, for use in World War II. She designed the machines which made the airplane parts, and trained the 4,500 workers in the plant. Elsie became so famous that, in 1942, a comic book was written about her. She was called the "Queen of the Hurricanes."

Elsie married the widower Bill Soulsby, who was the works manager at the plant. But workers weren't allowed to marry each other, so they were both fired. Elsie and Bill set up their own consulting company in Toronto, Ontario.

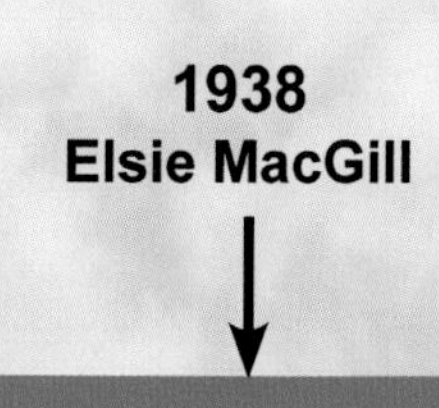

1900 **1910** **1920** **1930** **1940**

VI MILSTEAD
The first female bush pilot in Canada

Vi Milstead was born in Toronto, Ontario, in 1919. She wanted to be a surgeon, but her mother needed her help in their wool shop, so Vi left school. She decided to become a pilot instead of a doctor, and worked hard to earn enough money to pay for flying lessons. She took her lessons at 6 a.m. in order to be at the store on time. Vi earned her licence in 1939, after only four months of lessons.

During World War II, Vi flew airplanes in England with the Air Transport Auxiliary (ATA). She and other pilots who were not allowed to be combat pilots flew new planes from British factories to where the combat pilots were located. She also flew damaged planes to junk yards.

After the war ended, Vi returned to Canada. In 1947, she became Canada's first female bush pilot. She flew mine surveyors, trappers, lumberjacks, hunters, fishermen, and fire fighters to the bush in the Canadian north, where there were no roads, or where they had to get to quickly.

Her husband, Arnold Warren, was also a bush pilot.

DID YOU KNOW?

A postage stamp honouring Vi Milstead was issued Oct 17, 2009, on Vi's ninetieth birthday. It shows Vi in her ATA uniform.

1947
Vi Milstead

1950 1960 1970 1980 1990 2000

MARION ORR

The first Canadian woman to own an airport

Born in 1918, Marion Orr was from Toronto, Ontario. When she was young, she pretended she was flying an airplane when she played on her family swing. She was so fascinated by planes that she often walked six miles to an airport to watch airplanes take off and land.

Marion wanted to become a pilot so badly that she walked to work, and did without make-up, new clothes, and lunches to save money to pay for flying lessons. At that time, lessons cost $6.00 per hour, and were very expensive for her because her factory job only paid her $10.00 per week.

Marion took her test to get her pilot's licence on January 5, 1940. Her engine stopped when she was in the air, but she landed safely and passed. During World War II, she also flew airplanes in England with the Air Transport Auxiliary, just as Vi Milstead did.

In 1949, Marion bought her own airport at Barker field near Toronto, called Aero Activities Ltd., and became the first woman in Canada to own and operate a flying club. In 1954, she moved her airport to Maple, Ontario. There, she had seven instructors and ten airplanes. Marion taught over 5,000 men and women to fly.

In total, Marion flew almost 23,000 hours during her career, the equivalent of flying 24 hours a day for 2 ½ years.

1900 **1910** **1920** **1930** **1940**

Marion Orr.
Photo: Canada Aviation and Space Museum.

1949
Marion Orr

1950 **1960** **1970** **1980** **1990** **2000**

FELICITY BENNET MCKENDRY
Flying instructor

Felicity Bennet was born in 1929, and grew up on a farm in Spencerville, Ontario. When she drove her family's tractor, she pretended that she was flying a plane. She made balsa wood model aircraft, flying them with elastic bands. One year, she won first prize in the model aircraft section at the Spencerville Fair.

Felicity dreamed of becoming a pilot, but since very few women were allowed to fly, she decided to become a stewardess. Unfortunately, she grew too tall to become a stewardess, so she became a teacher instead.

Later, Felicity did learn how to fly, and got her pilot's licence in 1951. She became a well-known flying instructor, and taught many men and women to fly, even teaching Spence McKendry, the man who would become her husband. She also taught future Canadian astronauts, Marc Garneau and Steve McLean, to fly.

DID YOU KNOW?

A postage stamp to honour Felicity Bennet McKendry was released May 1, 2013. It celebrates the sixtieth anniversary of Felicity becoming a flight instructor.

1900 1910 1920 1930 1940

Felicity Bennet McKendry on her first day as a flying instructor in 1953.
Photo courtesy of George Lily, Kingston Whig-Standard.

1953
Felicity Bennet McKendry

1950 1960 1970 1980 1990 2000

ROSELLA BJORNSON

The first female pilot on a major airline in Canada

Born in 1947, Rosella Bjornson always wanted to be a pilot. When she was young, she played in an abandoned warplane without wings, pretending she was flying, with dolls as her passengers. When Rosella got older, she told the guidance counselor at her school in Lethbridge, Alberta, that she was going to be a pilot, but the guidance counselor laughed and said only boys could be pilots.

But Rosella did learn to fly. When she was very young, she sat on her father's knee in their family plane and he taught her about flying. Then, on July 13, 1964, when she was 17, her parents gave her a surprise birthday gift - flying lessons. She received her licence in a record two months.

In 1973, Rosella became the first female pilot to fly for a commercial airline in Canada – Transair Airlines. Then, in 1990, she became the first female captain on a scheduled airline in Canada – Canadian Airlines International.

✈

DID YOU KNOW?

A stamp to honour Rosella was issued on July 13, 2014, to celebrate the fiftieth anniversary of her first lesson.

1900 1910 1920 1930 1940

Rosella Bjornson in an airplane cockpit. You can see four stripes on her shoulder, indicating she is a captain.
Photo courtesy of Rosella Bjornson.

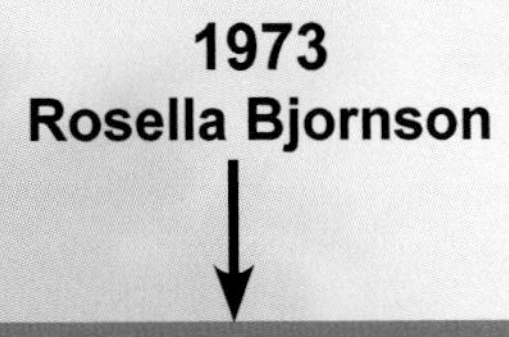

1950 **1960** **1970** **1980** **1990** **2000**

JUDY CAMERON

Air Canada's first female pilot

Born in 1954, Judy Cameron bought a motorcycle after university, which she and her mother rode because it was cheaper than driving a car. When Judy decided she wanted to be a pilot, she sold her motorcycle to pay for flying lessons.

Judy began her flying career as a bush pilot. At one time, she was based in the Canadian north, in Inuvik, Northwest Territories. She had to refuel her plane by jumping up on the wings where there were often many mosquitoes. She had to lift 45-gallon fuel drums. She often flew when the weather was below zero and visibility was poor. It was very hard work.

In 1978, Judy became the first female pilot with Air Canada. Her uniform was the same as the male pilot uniform, except she had an ascot instead of a tie. She also had a different hat, one with a little brim.

Judy flew with Air Canada for 37 years before retiring in 2015. During her career, she flew 23,000 hours, a record for female pilots.

✈

DID YOU KNOW?

There are about 3,100 pilots flying for Air Canada.
Of these, only about 160 are women.
That's about 5% women and 95% men.

1900 1910 1920 1930 1940

The first female pilot with Air Canada, Judy Cameron retired after flying with them for 37 years.
Photo: Rick Madonik/Get Stock.

1978
Judy Cameron

1950 **1960** **1970** **1980** **1990** **2000**

AKKY MANSIKKA
Skywatch pilot

Akky Mansikka, born in Holland in 1945, was eight when she came to Canada. She thought the coloured leaves in the fall were magical. Akky wanted to be a pilot, but had to wait until after she married and her children grew up.

Today, Akky is a pilot for Operation Skywatch, a program that began in Ontario in 1978. Skywatch pilots fly airplanes so the government photographers flying with them can take photos of pollution on the ground. The pilots must be women and members of the 99s, an international organization of women pilots. They must have a commercial pilot's licence and have flown for at least 1,000 hours.

Akky also flies small airplanes in Toronto, Ontario. On July 10, 2010, she flew a plane following the same route as that of the first airplane to fly over Toronto in July 1910. That plane was flown by a Frenchman, Count Jacques de Lesseps, who flew twenty miles.

✈

DID YOU KNOW?

There are laws against pollution in every province.
What are the laws in your province?
How can you find out?.

1900 1910 1920 1930 1940

Akky Mansikka prepares to fly.
Photo courtesy of Heather Bradacs.

1950 1960 1970 1980 1990 2000

MARY ELLEN PAULI
Helicopter bush pilot

Not all bush pilots fly airplanes. Some of them fly helicopters. Mary Ellen Pauli is a helicopter bush pilot.

Born in Matagami, Quebec, Mary Ellen dreamt of becoming a bush pilot like her father, but she had a difficult time. A company that trained helicopter pilots didn't want to train a woman. Then, when she finally did receive training, no company wanted to hire her because she was a woman. But Mary Ellen was determined and won out. In 1980, she got a job with Trans Quebec Helicopters because there were no male pilots available.

Mary Ellen currently flies with the Ministry of Natural Resources in northern Canada. She conducts environmental studies, such as counting moose from the air to see how many there are in Canada, and helping to track polar bears to see where they live and travel in the north.

While flying in the north, Mary Ellen has had many adventures. She had to frighten away polar bears from her camp, and once she rescued a family stranded on an island at the mouth of Hudson Bay, flying through sleet, strong winds and rain to save them.

✈

DID YOU KNOW?

The Bushplane Heritage Centre in Sault Ste. Marie has information and displays about Canadian bush pilots.

1900 1910 1920 1930 1940

Mary Ellen Pauli beside her helicopter.
Photo courtesy of Katelyn Malo.

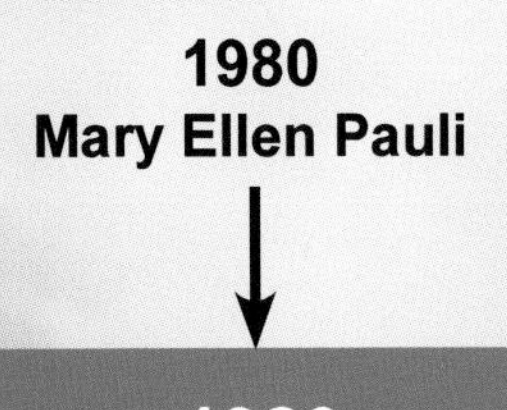

1950 1960 1970 1980 1990 2000

DEE BRASSEUR

One of the first two Canadian women to fly a fighter airplane

Born in 1953 in Pembroke, Ontario, Deanna (Dee) Brasseur thought that if she were a boy she would learn to fly a plane, because boys were allowed to be pilots.

When Dee was nineteen, she joined the military as a typist. There, she learned of a program called SWINTER (which stands for "Service Women in Non-Traditional Environment and Roles") encouraging women to fly. As a result, Dee became a pilot.

In 1981, Dee was one of three women in the military to get her wings. She also became the first woman to teach flying at the Canadian Forces Flying School in Moose Jaw, Saskatchewan.

In late 1988, Dee and Jane Foster became the first two women to fly a CF-18 jet fighter airplane. Dee flew at almost twice the speed of sound – 31.9 km per minute.

Today, Dee speaks to groups of people around the world. She helps men and women work towards doing their best wherever they are.

✈

DID YOU KNOW?

A stamp honouring Major Dee Brasseur, issued June 9, 2015, celebrates the anniversary of Dee's graduation as a pilot.

1900 1910 1920 1930 1940

Major Dee Brasseur, pilot of CF-18 fighter jets.
Photo courtesy of Department of National Defence (Canada).

1988
Dee Brasseur

1950 **1960** **1970** **1980** **1990** **2000**

ROBERTA BONDAR

The first Canadian female astronaut

Roberta Bondar was born in 1946 in Sault Ste. Marie, Ontario. She always wanted to be an astronaut. When she was young, she made models of rocket ships and space stations. When she was eleven, she made a model of "Sputnik," the first Russian satellite. Her mother kept it for 35 years, and gave it back to her when she became an astronaut.

A good athlete, Roberta also earned a degree in science, and then became a pilot. She wanted to become a doctor too, but at first her marks weren't good enough. She never gave up, studied hard, got a PhD in science, then became a doctor.

Because of all her knowledge and skills, Roberta was selected to be an astronaut, and became Canada's first female astronaut. She flew in the Space Shuttle "Discovery" in 1992, and was responsible for conducting over 40 experiments. She studied how plants grow in space. She observed how being in space affects people: how they become taller in space and have better eyesight, but when they come back to earth they become shorter and have to wear glasses.

Roberta was in the "Discovery" for more than eight days and went around the earth 129 times, crossing North America in ten minutes each time the shuttle orbited the earth.

Today, Roberta is a writer, and speaks to various groups of people.

DID YOU KNOW?

It takes ninety minutes for a space ship to go around the earth.

1900 1910 1920 1930 1940

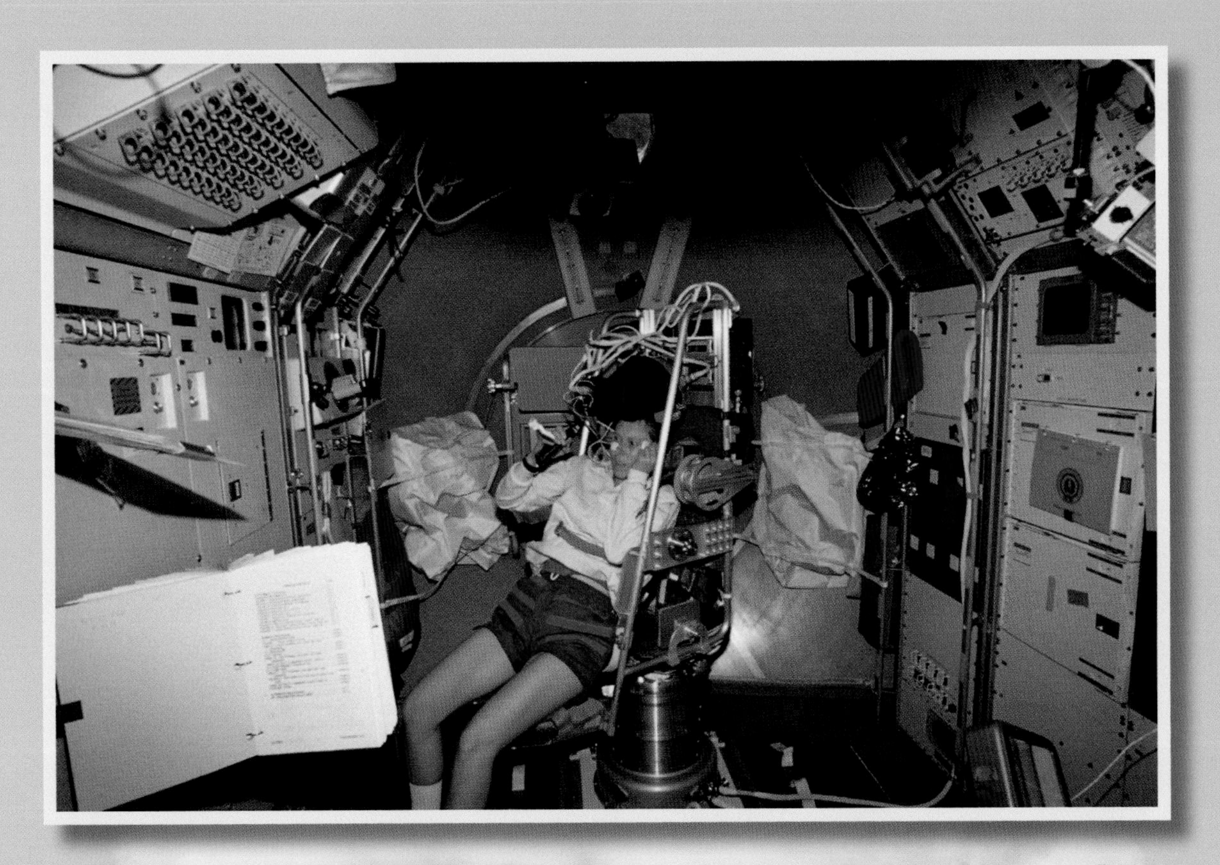

Roberta Bondar conducting experiments in the Space Shuttle "Discovery." Photo courtesy of NASA.

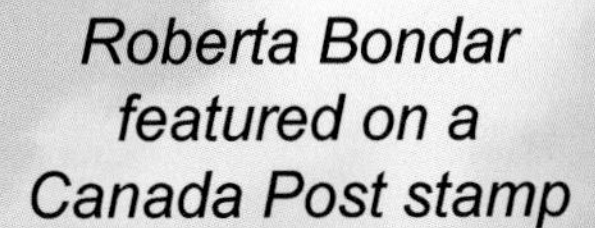

Roberta Bondar featured on a Canada Post stamp

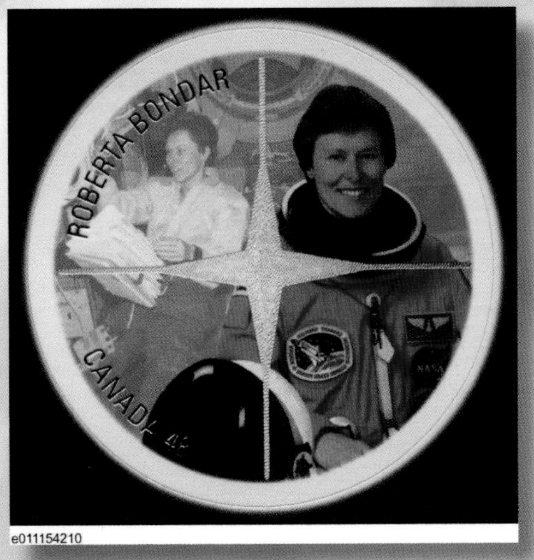

1992
Roberta Bondar

1950 1960 1970 1980 1990 2000

ADELE FOGLE

World flyer

The first time Adele flew solo, she crashed her small plane in front of dozens of observers. She wasn't frightened. She just decided that next time she'd do better. And she did.

Born in Toronto in 1924, the daughter of European immigrants, Adele didn't learn to fly until she was almost forty. Her first job flying an airplane was delivering newspapers and mail between Montreal and Toronto.

Eventually she bought an airport, Aviation International, in Guelph, Ontario, and operated it for twenty-five years.

Adele took part in many airplane races in small planes with other female pilot friends, even flying around the world over countries such as Morocco, Turkey, Dubai, Vietnam, Japan, Russia, and the United States. They had to land in some countries and refuel.

For a number of years, after 1998, she and Daphne Schiff, now a retired professor at York University, flew to countries in Africa for the non-profit programme, "Air Solidarité," to deliver medicine and school supplies they collected themselves. Adele and Daphne would fly to Paris to pick up a small plane from "Air Solidarité," then fly almost 4,000 miles to Africa. They also raised money for various projects in Africa, such as water purification plants, women's literacy programmes, schools, and health centres.

Adele loves flying because it's such a feeling of freedom.

1900 1910 1920 1930 1940

Adele Fogle beside the plane she flies.
Photo: Al Glbert C.M.

1998
Adele Fogle

1950 **1960** **1970** **1980** **1990** **2000**

JULIE PAYETTE

The first Canadian woman to enter the International Space Station

Julie Payette was born in 1963 in Montreal, Quebec, and wanted to become an astronaut. Julie made scrapbooks of space flights and, when she was nine, she decided to become an astronaut, even though she had never been in an airplane.

Julie loved sports, learned to play the piano, and sang in choirs. She speaks French, English, Spanish, and Italian and learned Russian to work in the space program.

Julie became an engineer before she was chosen to become an astronaut. Even then, she had to work and study for years to train to go up in space.

On May 27, 1999, Julie went up in the Space Shuttle "Discovery." The shuttle docked at the International Space Station forty hours after leaving the earth, and Julie became the first Canadian woman to enter the International Space Station. Julie supervised a spacewalk and operated the Canadarm.

In 2009, Julie went back into space, this time in the space shuttle "Endeavour." She was the flight engineer.

Julie now heads a Science Centre in Montreal, Quebec.

DID YOU KNOW?

When the space capsule went around the earth, it was 150°C above zero when in the sunlight, and 150°C below zero when they were out of the sunlight. It changed every 45 minutes.

1900 1910 1920 1930 1940

Julie Payette "flying" around in the space capsule.
Photo courtesy of NASA.

Canada Post stamp featuring Julie Payette

1999
Julie Payette

1950 **1960** **1970** **1980** **1990** **2000**

MARYSE CARMICHAEL
The first woman to fly with the Snowbirds

The Canadian Forces Snowbirds aerobatic team began in 1970 in Moose Jaw, Saskatchewan. The team of nine airplanes perform exciting shows, flying in thrilling formations. They travel around North America to demonstrate their skill.

It is not easy to become a Snowbird pilot. The pilots must be very skilled and experienced. They fly their planes at 650 km per hour while doing complicated formations, and must train every day. Snowbird pilots fly for only three years because it is a stressful and dangerous job.

Born in 1971, in Quebec City, Maryse Carmichael saw the Snowbirds in Bagotville, Quebec, when she was five years old. She never imagined that one day she would become a Snowbird pilot.

Maryse became an air cadet when she was thirteen. Within three years she learned how to fly gliders. When she was nineteen, Maryse joined the Canadian Armed Forces. She completed pilot training, and received her wings in 1994. There were only two women in her class of 140 people.

Maryse was chosen to fly with the Snowbirds in 2000. In 2010, Maryse became the first woman to be the commanding officer of the Snowbirds.

DID YOU KNOW?

Doug Farmer at Bushell Elementary School in Moose Jaw, Saskatchewan, won the contest to name the Snowbirds.

Snowbirds flying with an F86-Sabre. Photo courtesy of Royal Canadian Air Force.

1900 1910 1920 1930 1940

Maryse Carmichael in her Snowbirds uniform.
Photo courtesy of Royal Canadian Air Force.

2000
Maryse
Carmichael

1950 **1960** **1970** **1980** **1990** **2000**

The East Canada Chapter of the 99s

The international organization of women pilots, the Ninety-Nines or 99s, began in 1929. It was set up to support women pilots. The 99s offer scholarships, hold workshops, send out newsletters, sponsor air races, and maintain a museum.

The East Canada Chapter of the 99s organization has designed postage stamps of some Canadian women pilots. There are pictures of some stamps throughout this book, and others are shown here.

Dorothy Rungeling, from Fenwick, Ontario, born in 1911, was the first Canadian woman to fly in an international air race, from Florida to Windsor, in 1951. She was also the first Canadian woman to fly a helicopter by herself. The stamp was issued on May 12, 2010, her 99th birthday.

Isabel Peppler from Hanover, Ontario, born in 1934, was an airplane instructor. She published the first text book for student pilots in 1967, *From the Ground Up*. The stamp was issued in 2010.

Lorna de Blicquy from Blythe, Ontario, born in 1931, became the first female civil aviation inspector in Canada, in 1977. She was also the youngest Canadian woman to make a parachute jump, which she did when she was sixteen.

Aviation Museums in Canada

There are many aviation museums across Canada where we can see different types of airplanes, including:

North Atlantic Aviation Museum, Gander, Newfoundland
Atlantic Canada Aviation Museum, Halifax, Nova Scotia
Canadian Aviation Heritage Centre, Montréal, Québec
Canada Aviation and Space Museum, Ottawa, Ontario
Canadian Bushplane Heritage Centre, Sault Ste. Marie, Ontario
Royal Aviation Museum of Western Canada, Winnipeg, Manitoba
Saskatchewan Western Development Museum, Moose Jaw, Saskatchewan
Alberta Aviation Museum, Edmonton, Alberta
British Columbia Aviation Museum, Sidney, British Columbia

POSTAGE STAMPS - CREDITS

Roberta Bondar and Julie Payette postage stamps © Canada Post Corporation (2003), reproduced with permission. All other aviator stamps courtesy the East Canada Section of the Ninety-Nines (http://www.canadian99s.org), designed by Suzanne Wiltshire with the exception of Isabel Peppler, designed by Don Wong and permission to use granted by Graeme Peppler, Aviation Publishers Co Ltd.

IMPORTANT DATES

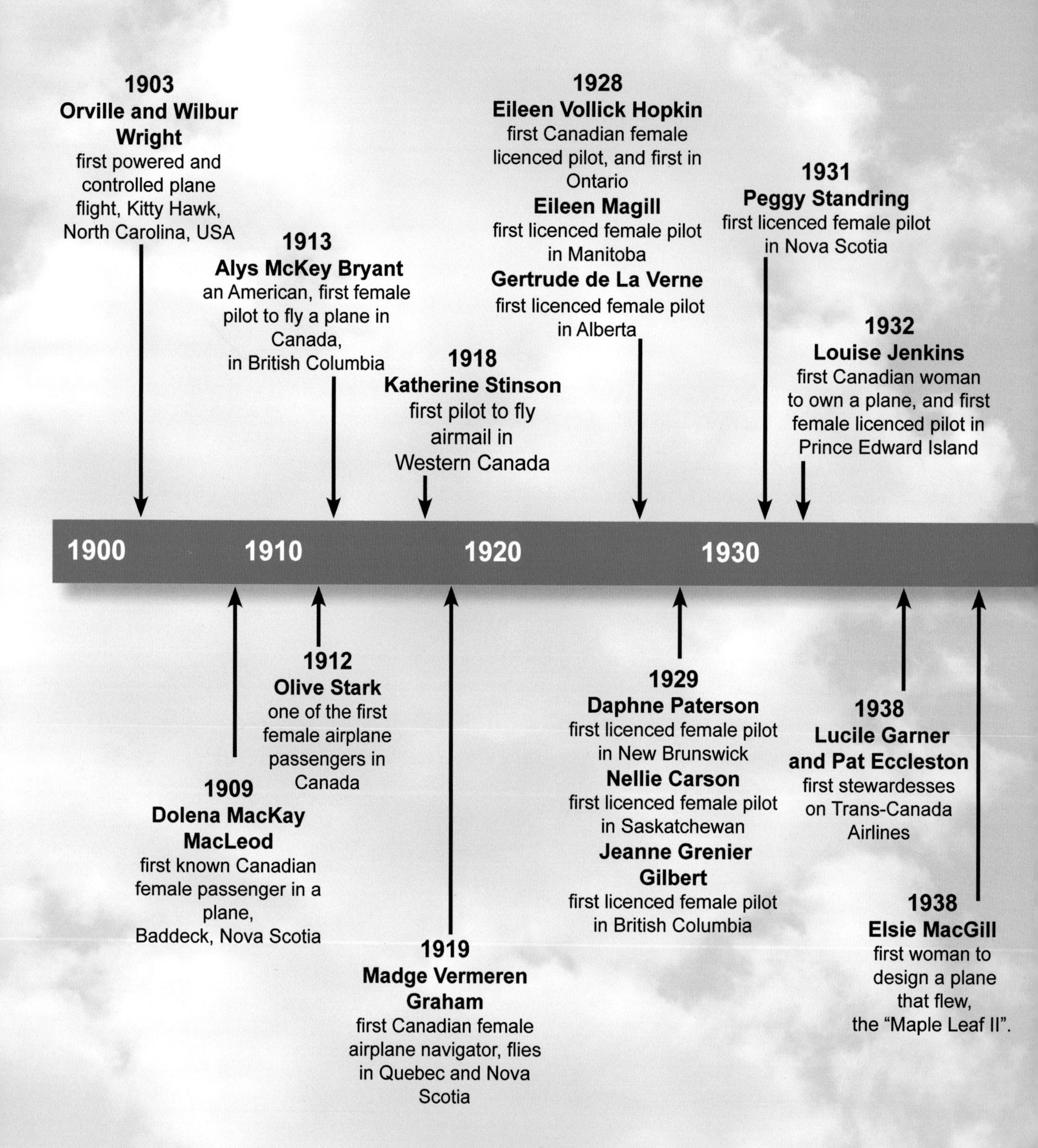

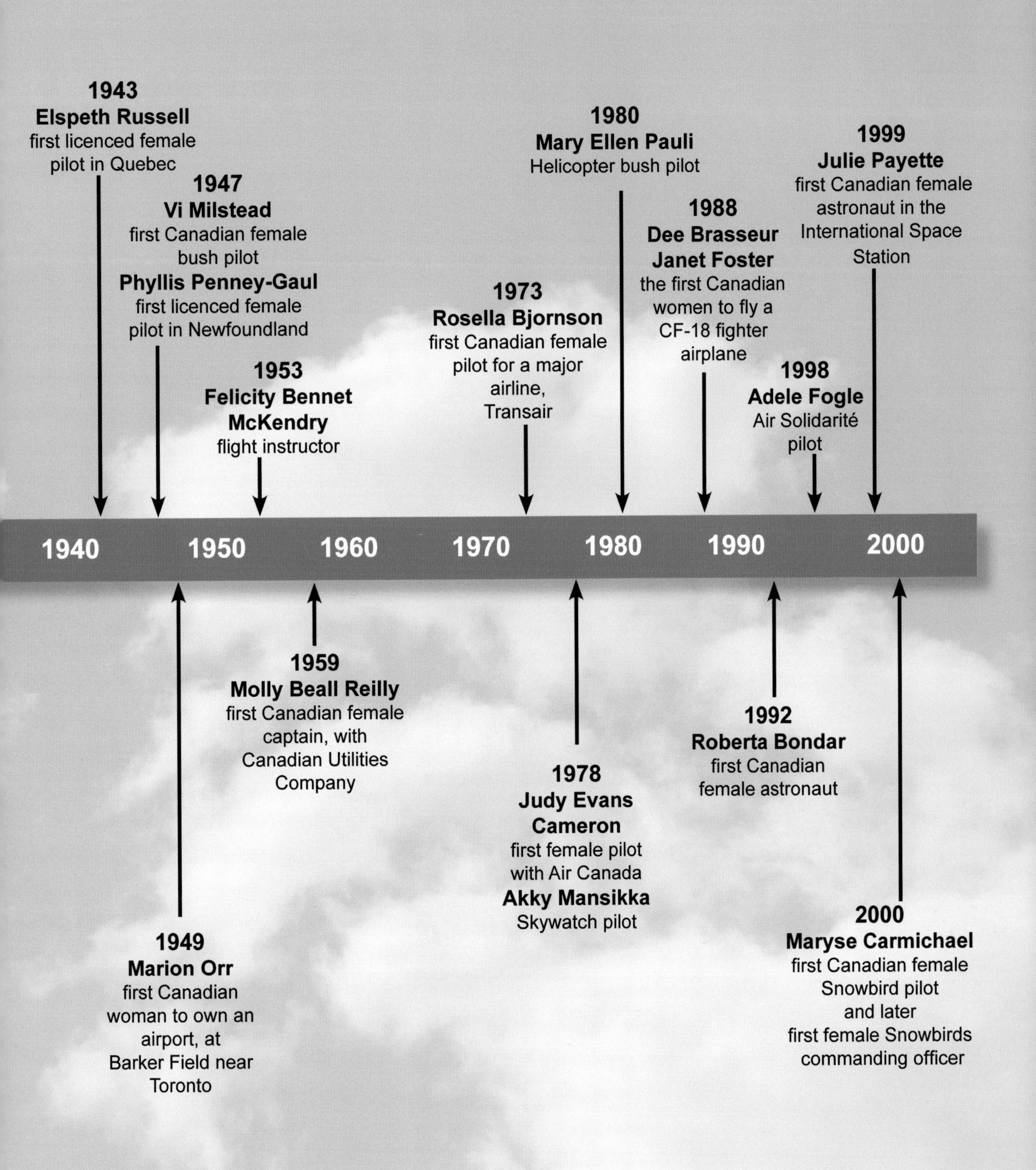

1943
Elspeth Russell
first licenced female pilot in Quebec
1947
Vi Milstead
first Canadian female bush pilot
Phyllis Penney-Gaul
first licenced female pilot in Newfoundland
1953
Felicity Bennet McKendry
flight instructor
1973
Rosella Bjornson
first Canadian female pilot for a major airline, Transair
1980
Mary Ellen Pauli
Helicopter bush pilot
1988
Dee Brasseur
Janet Foster
the first Canadian women to fly a CF-18 fighter airplane
1998
Adele Fogle
Air Solidarité pilot
1999
Julie Payette
first Canadian female astronaut in the International Space Station
1940
1950
1960
1970
1980
1990
2000
1949
Marion Orr
first Canadian woman to own an airport, at Barker Field near Toronto
1959
Molly Beall Reilly
first Canadian female captain, with Canadian Utilities Company
1978
Judy Evans Cameron
first female pilot with Air Canada
Akky Mansikka
Skywatch pilot
1992
Roberta Bondar
first Canadian female astronaut
2000
Maryse Carmichael
first Canadian female Snowbird pilot and later first female Snowbirds commanding officer

ELIZABETH (LIZ) GILLAN MUIR

Elizabeth (Liz) Gillan Muir, an historian and author in Toronto, has written stories for children's magazines in Canada, the United States, Australia, and Great Britain. She was paid $1.00 for her first story, "Marsh Hens", which was published in *Child Life* when she was ten. She has recently published two adult books: *Riverdale: east of the Don* and *Canadian Women in the Sky: 100 years of flight*.

Liz is grateful to those women in this book who gave her tremendous support and encouragement, and to the publisher of Another Chapter Publishing, Roxanne McLaren, who contributed enormous skill, patience, and enthusiasm.